Keyboard Classics

**9 well-known pieces for piano
by one of the world's greatest composers**

TABLE OF CONTENTS

All selections on the CD are
performed by Chie Nagatani except
"Ecossaise in E♭," "Ecossaise in G" and
"Theme from Rondo a Capriccio," which are
performed by Kim O'Reilly.

ISBN 0-7390-1722-5

Copyright © MMI Alfred Publishing Co., Inc.
All rights reserved. Printed in USA.

Cover photo: © Horst Klemm / Masterfile

Ludwig van Beethoven

Ludwig van Beethoven was born in Bonn, Germany, on December 16, 1770. He died March 26, 1827, in Vienna. His grandfather had been the Kapellmeister for the Archbishop, and his father was a court musician. But his father was also the town drunk, and he was cruel to his son. If Ludwig did not practice enough to please his father, he was beaten. He saw that Ludwig had remarkable talent and was determined to capitalize on it by exploiting him as a child prodigy. This might have adversely affected the love for music of a child less gifted. But the young Beethoven lived and breathed music and soon became a brilliant pianist and a master of improvisation. His first work was published when he was only 11 years old, and others followed very quickly.

Although he did go through periods of financial want during his lifetime, for the most part his compositions brought him a considerable income, so that he did have reasonable security. On one occasion, he lacked enough money to pay his rent. A friend dropped in, and Beethoven told him of his problem. "I cannot understand that," said the friend. "After all, you are Beethoven." With that the friend gave Beethoven a short theme and told him to write some variations. In a short time, the work was finished. The friend went out for a few moments and returned with a good sum of money. . . more than enough for the emergency. He had sold the theme and variations to a publisher a short distance down the street!

When he was 17 years old, Beethoven traveled to Vienna. Here he made a great impression on everyone who heard him play, and especially on those who heard his improvisations. Even Mozart said, "Keep an eye on that fellow; he will make a great commotion in the world some day!" When he was 22 years old, Beethoven moved to Vienna where he remained for most of the remainder of his life. He achieved great fame as a pianist and as a composer. His new works were eagerly awaited by a large circle of musicians who especially appreciated his genius. On one occasion, they even signed a petition requesting that a new work be given public performance. That work was his great 9th Symphony, composed for orchestra and chorus.

The great tragedy of Beethoven's life was his deafness, which shut him off from society for the last half of his life. He was unable to hear his music performed but could hear it perfectly in his own mind. His sense of pitch and quality of sound did not disappear when his hearing vanished, and his greatest works were composed when he was almost totally deaf. It has been suggested that his deafness may have been a blessing, since it caused him to withdraw from society to such an extent that he had a great deal of time to compose. It also caused him to become philosophical and introspective, and one can hear this in his music. As he composed his great 5th Symphony, he said, "I will seize fate by the throat. . . I will not be defeated." And this work was his symphony of victory, indeed.

Not only did Beethoven revolutionize the symphony as a musical form, but he totally changed the direction of music in general. He ushered in a new era for the piano. Even his "trifles" (Bagatelles) were the beginning of a vast new literature of short piano pieces of a similar type.

Ecossaise in E♭

WoO 86

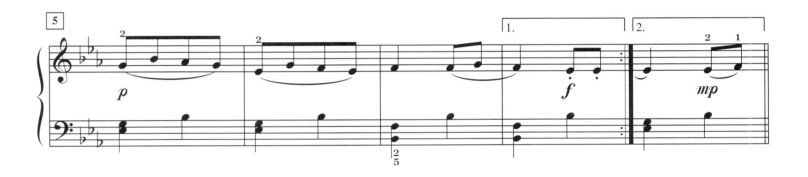

Ecossaise in G

 Track 2

WoO 23

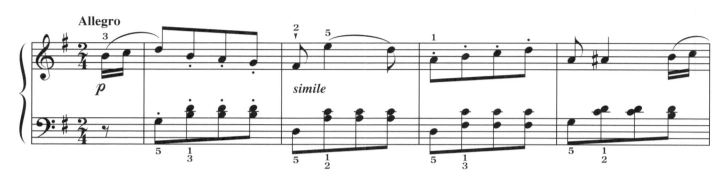

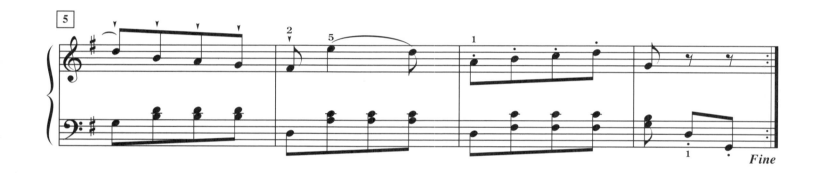

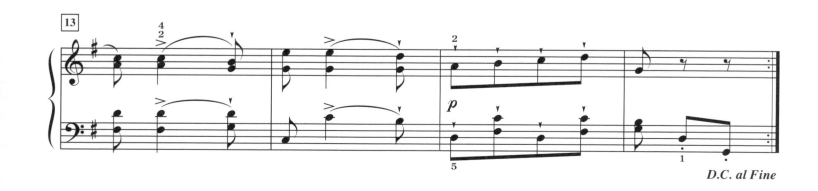

D.C. al Fine

Turkish March

from *The Ruins of Athens*

 Track 3

Op. 113, No. 4

Für Elise

WoO 59

Track 4

*In most modern editions, this note appears as a D instead of an E (here and in subsequent similar passages). In the original edition and in the only known Beethoven autograph sketch, the note appears as an E throughout the composition.

Menuet in G Major

WoO 10, No. 2

Track 5

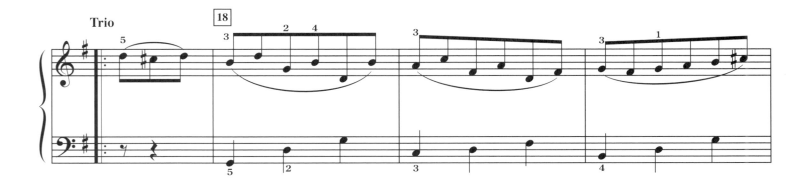

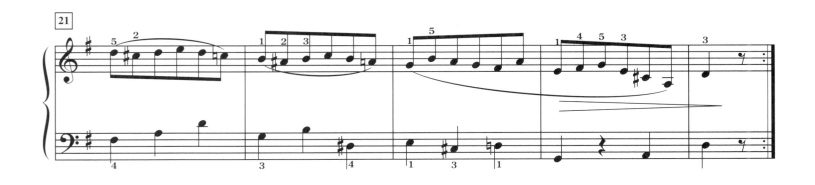

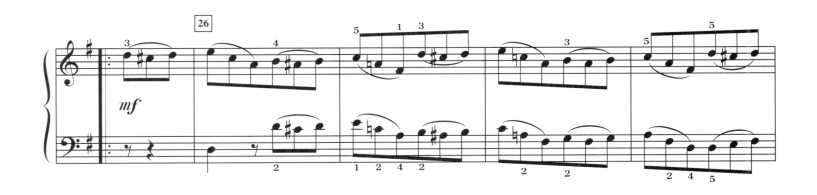

Menuet da Capo

Sonata Quasi una Fantasia

("Moonlight Sonata")
1st Movement

Track 6

Op. 27, No. 2

Adagio sostenuto

Very delicately, with pedal throughout.

*Beethoven's own instructions.

16

Sonata Pathetique
2nd Movement

Track 7

Op. 13

Theme from Rondo a Capriccio

("Rage over the Lost Penny")

 Track 8

Op. 129

*Alla ingharese, quasi un capriccio

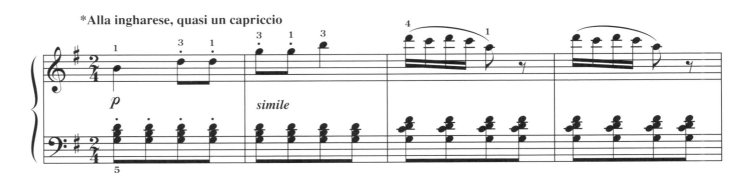

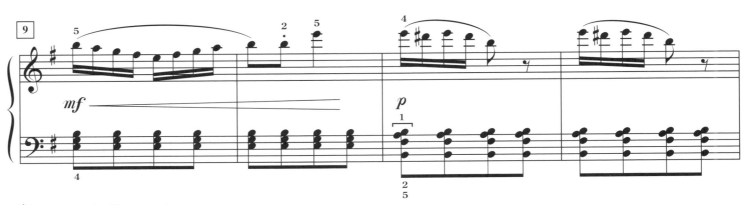

*In gypsy style, like a caprice.

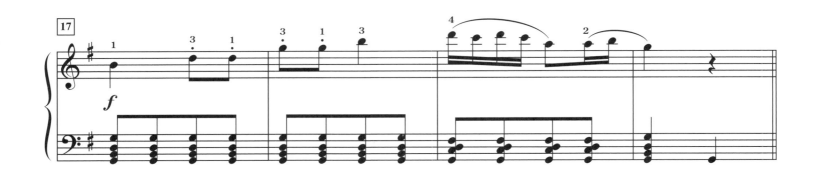

This page has been intentionally left blank to facilitate page turns.

Contradance

WoO 14, No. 1

Track 9

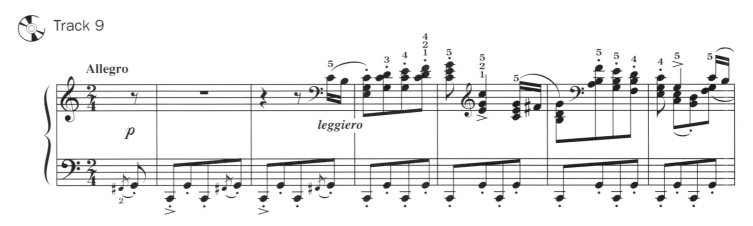